D0177649

10001737163 4

The Making of a Champion

A World-Class Swimmer

Heinemann
LIBRARY

Paul Mason

Solihull
LIBRARIES & ARTS

H **www.heinemann.co.uk/library**
Visit our website to find out more information about **Heinemann Library** books.

To order:
☎ Phone 44 (0) 1865 888066
🗎 Send a fax to 44 (0) 1865 314091
💻 Visit the Heinemann Bookshop at www.heinemann.co.uk/library to browse our catalogue and order online.

First published in Great Britain by Heinemann Library, Halley Court, Jordan Hill, Oxford OX2 8EJ, part of Harcourt Education. Heinemann is a registered trademark of Harcourt Education Ltd.

© Harcourt Education Ltd 2004
The moral right of the proprietor has been asserted.

All rights reserved. No part of this publication may be reproduced, stored in a retrieval system, or transmitted in any form or by any means, electronic, mechanical, photocopying, recording, or otherwise, without either the prior written permission of the publishers or a licence permitting restricted copying in the United Kingdom issued by the Copyright Licensing Agency Ltd, 90 Tottenham Court Road, London W1T 4LP (www.cla.co.uk).

Editorial: Andrew Farrow and Dan Nunn
Design: David Poole and Geoff Ward
Illustrations: Geoff Ward
Picture Research: Rebecca Sodergren and Fiona Orbell
Production: Viv Hichens

Originated by Ambassador Litho Ltd
Printed in China by WKT Company Limited

ISBN 0 431 18922 6
08 07 06 05 04
10 9 8 7 6 5 4 3 2 1

British Library Cataloguing in Publication Data
Mason, Paul
A World-Class Swimmer - (The Making of a Champion)
1. Swimming - Juvenile literature
2. Swimming - Training - Juvenile literature
I. Title
797.2'1
A full catalogue record for this book is available from the British Library.

Acknowledgements
The publishers would like to thank the following for permission to reproduce photographs:

Action Plus pp. **9 top**, **10**, **11 bottom** (Glyn Kirk), **13**, **21 bottom** (Glyn Kirk), **36**, **39 top**; Corbis pp. **7 top** (Jerry Cooke), **9 bottom** (Bettmann), **11 top** (Joseph Sohm/ChromoSohm Inc.), **43 top** (Hulton-Deutsch Collection), **43 bottom** (Duomo/Paul J. Sutton); Empics pp. **16** (Steve Mitchell), **18 left** (Michael Steele), **22** (Michael Steele), **23 top** (Matthew Ashton), **40**, **41 bottom**; L'Equipe pp. **4**, **5 bottom**, **6 top**, **17**, **20**, **25 bottom**, **26**, **27 left**, **27 right**, **34**, **35 bottom**, **38** (Tony Marshall), **39 bottom**; Getty Images pp. **8**, **18 right**, **19**, **25 top**, **29**, **31**, **35 top**; Getty News and Sport pp. **37** (Shaun Botterill), **42**; Harcourt Education Ltd p. **32** (Trevor Clifford); Hulton Getty p. **7 bottom**; PA Photos/EPA pp. **12**, **21 top**; Reuters pp. **5 top** (Ian Waldie), **6 bottom** (David Gray), **14** (Alexander Demianchuk), **23 bottom** (Mark Baker), **28** (Kimimasa Mayama), **30** (David Gray), **33** (Will Burgess), **41 top** (Marcelo Del Pozo); Sporting Pictures UK Ltd p. **15** (Simon Miles).

Cover photograph reproduced with permission of Action Plus/Neil Tingle.

Every effort has been made to contact copyright holders of any material reproduced in this book. Any omissions will be rectified in subsequent printings if notice is given to the publishers.

⬛⬛⬛⬛	
CL1OOO1737163 4	
Askews	
J797.2	⬛⬛⬛
	L7580

Contents

Words printed in bold letters, **like these**, are explained in the Glossary.

An Olympic final

Sydney, 16 September 2000: The Olympic pool is packed with over 15,000 spectators, every one of them at a fever pitch of excitement. For months before this first day of Olympic swimming competition all the talk has been about the rivalry between the USA and Australia. These two countries are the strongest swimming nations in the world, but which will turn out to be the best?

Swimmers dive into the pool at the start of the 4 x 100m freestyle relay at the Sydney 2000 Olympics. It was to be one of the competition's most exciting races for years.

Grudge match

The competition has started well for the Australians. Their star swimmer, Ian Thorpe – otherwise known as 'the Thorpedo' – has already won the 400m freestyle in world-record time. Now the Thorpedo is back in action, as part of the 4 x 100m freestyle relay. This is a grudge match: before the race, the American 100m specialist Gary Hall Jnr had promised that the US team would 'smash the Australians like guitars'. Hall is due to race the final leg of the relay, against the Thorpedo.

The Australian team gets a fantastic start from Michael Klim, who sets a world-record time on his first leg of the relay. However, the Americans slowly begin to claw back ground. Thorpe dives into the pool for the final 100 metres of the race just ahead of Hall. The Americans seem certain to win – Thorpe specializes in longer distances, and Hall is one of the world's best 100m freestyle swimmers.

'The Thorpedo'

Name:	Ian Thorpe
Country:	Australia
State:	New South Wales
Club:	S.L.C. Aquadot
Born:	1982
Height:	195 cm
Weight:	102 kg
Place of birth:	Sydney
Occupation:	Swimmer
Coach:	Tracey Menzies
Interests:	Going to the movies, computer games

In 2002, Thorpe was the world-record holder for the 200m, 400m and 800m freestyle events.

Fight to the finish

As so often happens in swimming, things didn't go according to script. After the turn at 50 metres, Hall edged up level with Thorpe. The crowd, mainly Australians, sat forward on their seats. Then Thorpe's huge feet began to kick up a bubble of foaming water that looked as though it was coming from a propeller.

The Thorpedo torpedoed ahead of Hall, touching the wall first and helping the team to another world record. One of the other Australians leapt up onto the starting blocks and began playing an air guitar...

US revenge

On the last day of swimming the Americans got their revenge, beating Australia in the other big relay race, the 4 x 100m medley. They set a world-record time, helped on the final leg of the race by none other than Gary Hall Jnr. Gary himself certainly felt that the other team had helped his team set the record: 'When faced with a worthy opponent, you're forced to get your act together. We were able to reach a level we might not otherwise have reached.'

US star Gary Hall Jnr catches his breath after a race at the Sydney 2000 Olympics.

Competitive swimming

There are many different kinds of race in competitive swimming today, from long-distance open-water **endurance** competitions to short, 50m sprint races that are held in indoor pools. The measure of success in all of these is speed: no one gets points for style, only for finishing in front of other people.

Championship pools

Most races at competitions such as the Olympic Games and the World Championships are held indoors, in specially built racing pools. These have special 'lane lines' dividing the swimmers, as well as starting blocks and timing pads at each end. The timing pads are connected to a computer – when the swimmers finish, the computer works out who has won and how fast they have swum.

Special lane lines stop the turbulence from one swimmer affecting another.

Competitors in the 1999 Asian Games women's 200m backstroke final launch themselves from the blocks at the start of the race.

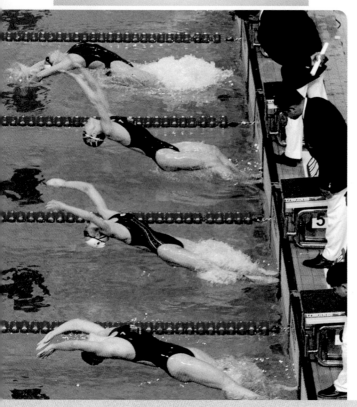

Different strokes

There are four strokes in modern competitive swimming: front crawl, backstroke, breaststroke and butterfly. Front crawl races are often called 'freestyle' events – in theory you can do any stroke in a freestyle race, but everyone uses front crawl because it's the fastest. As well as races featuring just one of these four strokes (100m breaststroke, for example) there are medley races. In a 200m medley race, each swimmer does 50 metres each of butterfly, backstroke, breaststroke and front crawl. As well as individual events, swimmers sometimes race in relays. This is where they take it in turns to swim part of the race.

Different distances

Swimming races take place over distances of 50, 100, 200, 400, 800 and 1500 metres. Longer distances – 400 metres and more – are almost always freestyle races. The only exception is the 400m medley, where the racers swim 100 metres of each stroke.

Sprint events are those that take place over 50 or 100 metres. Races of 200 and 400 metres are usually thought of as middle distance. Long-distance races are over 800 metres and 1500 metres.

The greatest Olympian?

Born in 1950 in Modesto, California, USA, Mark Spitz was one of the most successful Olympic competitors ever. At the 1968 Mexico Olympics, Spitz won two gold medals, a silver and a bronze while still a teenager. But his greatest Olympic performance was still to come.

In 1972 at the Munich Olympics, Spitz won seven gold medals. Four were for individual races – the 100m and 200m events at both butterfly and freestyle. The other three golds were in relays – the 400m and 800m freestyle, and the 400m medley. Each of the seven races was won in a world-record time.

One of the all-time great swimmers was a Hawaiian named Duke Kahanamoku. Duke won gold medals for freestyle at the 1912 and 1920 Olympics. His times were so quick that he smashed the world-record time along a measured course in Honolulu harbour. However, officials refused to accept the new record because they said it was too fast to be real!

Getting started

People get into competitive swimming in lots of different ways, but how you get into swimming depends partly on where you live. In Australia, for example, young children might want to join 'Nippers' groups that are part of surf lifesaving clubs. In Europe, most children get into swimming through swimming lessons at school. In the USA and Canada keen swimmers might join amateur clubs to develop their skills.

Making sacrifices

Wherever swimmers live, they all have one thing in common. If they want to become a champion, they will have to make sacrifices. Becoming a champion swimmer demands a lot of dedication, and doesn't leave much time for anything else. Staying up late, lie-ins, weekend jobs – many of the things that are part of being a teenager become impossible, because the training is so demanding.

Club swimming

Once a young person decides they want to become a competitive swimmer, it's time to join a swimming club. Most cities and many towns have swimming clubs: they are easy to find by contacting the local public pool. At a swimming club, racers get the help of a qualified coach. He or she will plan their training **sessions**, give advice on developing a good **technique**, and help them do better dives and turns.

Club members also take part in local championships and competitions with other clubs. Doing well in a local championship often qualifies you to race in a regional competition, then perhaps a national one and then even an international one. Even Olympic gold medallists begin their swimming careers by trying to win small local races!

These children are members of an Australian surf lifesaving club's 'Nippers' group. They are learning about water safety.

Joining a club

When new swimmers first go along to a club, they are usually given some sort of swimming test to find out how good they are. This is because the coaches need to know if the swimmer has reached a high-enough standard to train with them. If not, they may suggest having more lessons elsewhere before joining. If the swimmer is ready to join, the coaches need to decide which training group he or she is going to be in. The test helps them decide this.

These swimmers at a club training session are being carefully watched by their coach. Coaches play a vital role in developing a young swimmer's techniques and race strategies.

Training group fact

Most swimming clubs divide swimmers into groups depending on how fast they are. Sometimes the groups train together at the same time, but in different lanes. At bigger clubs the groups may be so big that they fill a whole pool, and have to train at different times.

Shane Gould

Shane Gould of Australia was one of the stars of the pool at the 1972 Olympics in Munich, West Germany. Gould won three gold medals and set world records in each event. Altogether, she swam twelve races in eight days – and all before her sixteenth birthday! However, Gould became fed up with the amount of training necessary to maintain her high position in the sport and, less than a year after her Olympic success, she retired. All her international competition was crammed into less than three years.

Equipment

Ten years ago there was very little choice about what to wear for swimming. Men wore trunks, which were skin-tight and fastened with a drawstring at the waist. Women wore one-piece costumes that were cut high on the legs, left the arms free to move easily and were usually slightly open at the back. Today, there is a bit more choice!

New costumes

Many racers now wear full-body suits made of special fabric. The makers claim that this fabric helps racers to swim faster, by creating a layer of air bubbles between the swimmer and the water. This allows faster times by reducing **turbulence** (disturbance of the water, which slows the swimmer down). Before these suits were invented, male and female swimmers used to shave off all their body hair to try to achieve a similar effect!

Hat and goggles

Practically all competition swimmers wear goggles. These help them see their opponents during a race, as well as helping them see their own **technique** in training. Most swimmers also wear a tight-fitting rubbery 'hat' or 'cap' that stretches over their head, reducing **resistance** from their hair as it drags in the water.

These swimmers are wearing a variety of costumes, but most have chosen full-body suits in one form or another.

Training aids

Swimmers use two different types of float to help them train. The first is a kickboard. They hold this out in front of them to do a legs-only version of a stroke. Legs-only swimming helps racers to develop their leg and stomach muscles, as well as giving them a chance to develop their kicking technique. The other type of float is a pull-buoy. This is tucked between a swimmer's thighs, and helps keep the back part of their body afloat as they do an arms-only version of a stroke.

Hand paddles are also widely used in swimming. These are sheets of plastic that swimmers strap to the palms of their hands. Paddles help develop strength in the muscles and improve stroke technique.

Kickboards like these are a useful training aid used by many swimmers to develop kicking technique.

Keeping warm

There is a lot of waiting around at swimming competitions, and it is important for swimmers to keep warm while they wait. Otherwise they can get cramp (a painful tightening of their muscles) or suffer injuries to cold muscles during their race. Keeping warm also stops swimmers from losing valuable energy by getting cold.

This German swimmer is wearing a tracksuit to keep warm before her big race. Some swimmers even wear hats to keep the heat in.

Full-body swimsuits fact

The fabric used in full-body swimsuits is based on sharkskin, which is made up of lots of tiny, tooth-like scales. The 'teeth' point backwards, and are layered on top of one another like the tiles on a roof. Swimsuit designers saw that a fabric like this might be of benefit to competition swimmers, and a revolution in swimwear began!

Front crawl

All strokes are made up of two parts: arm stroke and leg kick. Front crawl is the fastest stroke. In front crawl the basic **technique** is for the legs to kick constantly while each arm **pulls** in turn. As one arm is pulling under water, the other arm is going through the air above the water's surface, back to its starting position stretched out in front of the swimmer.

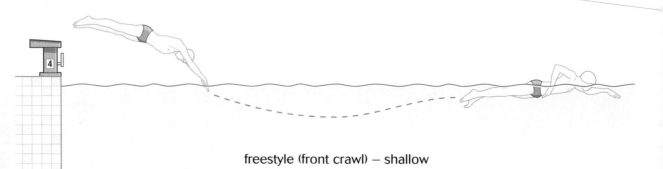

freestyle (front crawl) – shallow

The dive for a front crawl race should not be too deep. A shallow dive that lets the swimmer 'burst' up to the surface is best. Sprinters usually try to take several strokes before they breathe after diving in. This is because breathing creates turbulence and slows them down. It's best to get into the rhythm of the stroke before disturbing it by breathing.

Different techniques

While watching an Olympic swimming final on TV you might see two or three different styles of front crawl. Some athletes swim with a straight-arm **recovery**, while others have a very bent elbow. A swimmer's head position, the side they take a breath from, and their underwater pull can all be slightly varied.

Benko breaks record!

On the final day of competition at the January 2003 World Cup swimming meet, American Lindsay Benko finally broke Janet Evans's fourteen-year-old world record for 400m freestyle. She also became the first woman to swim the distance in under 4 minutes, clocking a time of 3:59.53. This achievement also won her a prize of US$20,000 and a brand-new car!

Underwater stroke

As the swimmer's arm enters the water their hand usually turns outwards slightly and briefly pulls away from the body. The swimmer then brings his or her arm back in under the body, pulling slightly across it at about chest level. Their hand then comes back to exit the water at about hip level. Overall, their hand makes a sort of 'S' shape.

Recovery

The recovery is the part of the stroke that brings the hands back to their starting places, ready to pull through the water again. Most coaches teach their swimmers to make a freestyle recovery with their arm bent at the elbow. The swimmer's hand comes through below the level of the elbow, just above the surface of the water. Then it slips back into the water, thumb and forefinger first.

At the end of each length (except the last one), front crawl racers use tumble turns. Just as their hand is about to touch the wall they whip it under their body, followed by their head, body and legs all tucked up into a neat shape. Their legs flip over and their feet hit the wall, ready to shove off for the next length. Racers try not to breathe for one or two strokes after the turn.

Leg kick

Front crawl leg kick is done with the toes pointing backwards and the legs almost straight. Swimmers kick with a movement of their hips and knees, but try not to rock their body from side to side – lots of little kicks are faster than a few big ones. Sprinters may do six kicks for each arm stroke; distance racers might do only two. If you watch any top swimmers as they come into the finish, the splash from their legs will probably be huge as they squeeze out the last bit of energy and speed.

Butterfly

Butterfly is like front crawl, but instead of the arms and legs working alternately, they do the same movements at the same time. When the arms are pulling, the swimmer's face is underwater, making the whole thing pretty exhausting!

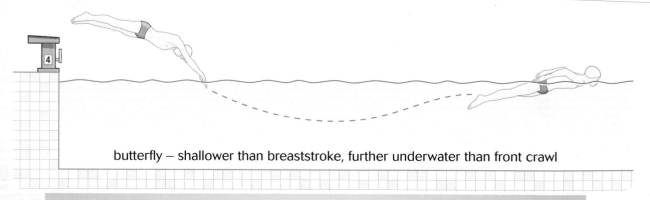

butterfly – shallower than breaststroke, further underwater than front crawl

Butterfly swimmers often dive in a bit deeper than front crawl racers. This is because their underwater leg kick can be as fast as their surface full stroke. But they have to be careful – swimming without taking a breath means their muscles are using up oxygen that isn't being replaced, so they risk running out of puff before the end of the race!

Arm stroke

Butterfly swimmers use an overarm **recovery**, like front crawl. But both arms come through the air at the same time with the elbows slightly bent. The hands meet when they are stretched out in front of the swimmer's body. Then the swimmer pulls his or her hands back and slightly away, before quickly pulling them back in and underneath their body. Just before the hands meet at about stomach level they come outwards again, exiting the water at about hip level.

Butterfly arm stroke requires swimmers to have flexible shoulders, as this shot of Australian swimmer Petria Thomas shows. Butterfly also demands the highest level of fitness, as it is extremely tiring.

Butterfly swimmers must touch the wall with both hands at the same time. Their hands must also be at the same height on the end of the pool. As soon as their hands touch, most swimmers drop their right arm and shoulder backwards and downwards. As they 'fall' away from the wall they bring their legs through under their body until their feet touch the wall. By now their body has twisted and their other arm has come back into the water. They are on their side facing back down the pool, ready to push off for the next length.

Leg kick

If you watch butterfly swimmers in a top-level race, you'll see that they kick their legs with their knees and ankles held lightly together. The kick starts at the hips, and is like a kind of wiggle that travels down the legs and ends at the feet. Racers do two kicks per arm stroke: a strong kick as their face comes out of the water after breathing, and another kick at the end of their arm pull.

Timing

The fastest butterfly swimmers time their leg kicks perfectly with their arm strokes. Timing the two parts of the stroke together is the key to swimming butterfly well; it also makes it much less tiring.

Underwater fact

Russian swimmer Denis Pankratov, 100m and 200m butterfly Olympic champion in 1996, broke several 50m butterfly world records by spending the entire race underwater! This made the race very boring to watch, so a change in the rules was made, saying that swimmers could only spend 15 metres underwater after starts and turns. This meant the spectators had something to watch again, and ensured that butterfly didn't become an entirely underwater stroke!

Breaststroke

Breaststroke is a dynamic, exciting stroke to watch. The swimmers power forwards underwater, then emerge to lunge ahead before their next leg kick drives them forwards again. The timing of the kick and **pull** is crucial to swimming breaststroke fast – most of the speed comes from the kick. The pull is partly used to add speed and partly to get the swimmer's body into position for the next kick.

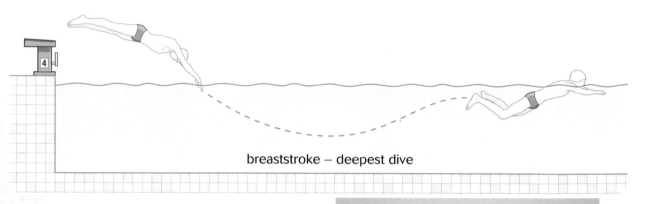

breaststroke – deepest dive

Arm stroke

Breaststroke arm strokes divide into three parts. First is the arm stroke itself, which moves the swimmer forward and lifts their head and shoulders out of the water. Second is the movement forward that brings their arms back to the starting point. Third is a glide, with the hands out in front and the arms straight. Great breaststroke sprinters like Zoe Baker of England, the 2002 world-record holder for **short-course** 50m breaststroke, usually have a short glide, and use a rapid arm stroke to power themselves along.

Breaststroke swimmers are allowed to take one arm stroke and one leg kick underwater before they come to the surface. Because of this they usually dive deeper than any other racers, and use their underwater strokes to get back up to the surface.

James Hickman of England, during the breaststroke leg of the 2000 World Cup men's 200m individual medley. The photo clearly shows how a powerful breaststroke arm action can lift a swimmer's body way above the surface of the water.

Leg kick

From overhead, a breaststroke leg kick looks a bit like that of a frog. Swimmers pull their feet up to their bottom, then turn their feet outwards and kick out sideways and back. As their feet come together at the end of the stroke, their toes are stretched out away from them, like a ballet dancer on point. This happens just as the arm stroke finishes too, so the swimmer glides forwards until the moment their speed is about to drop. The great swimmers of 200m breaststroke, like the 1976 Olympic champion David Wilkie, use this glide to conserve energy through the race, pacing themselves so that the last burst of energy is spent as they approach the finish.

Profile of a champion

Name:	Amanda Beard
Country:	USA
Born:	29 October 1981
Height:	173 cm
Trains:	Irvine, California
Club:	Irvine Novas

One of Beard's most exciting races was the 200m breaststroke at the World Championships in Barcelona, Spain, in 2003. Pitched against 'Lethal' Leisel Jones of Australia, Beard was behind at every turn. Down the last length Jones began to tire, perhaps after the effort of setting a new world record in the 100m four days earlier. Their epic battle helped Beard to win in a time that equalled the world record set by Qui Hi of China two years earlier – 2:22.99.

Turns

Breaststroke turns are basically very similar to butterfly turns (see page 15). The difference is that, as with the start, the racers are allowed to take one arm stroke and one leg kick underwater after their turn.

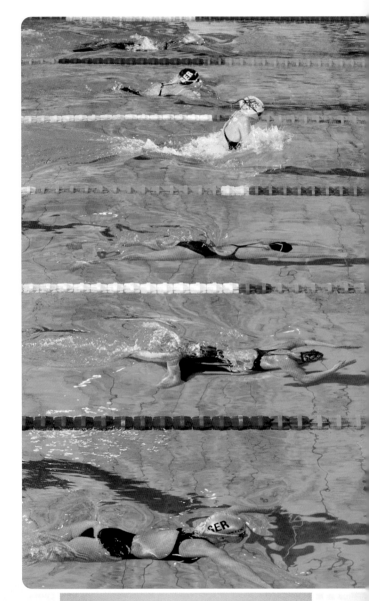

These swimmers are just coming to the surface after a start. Racers have different approaches to this: some, like the third swimmer from the top, like to get into their swimming early. Others, like the two swimmers below her, stay underwater for as long as possible.

Backstroke

Backstroke is the odd-man-out of swimming, because it's the only stroke in which the swimmers can't see where they're going. Backstroke swimmers navigate their way down the pool using the roof, half-caught glimpses of their lane line, and ropes that are specially placed across the pool 5 metres from each end.

Backstroke technique

Just as in front crawl, backstroke swimmers use first one arm then the other. As one shoulder and arm stretch through the underwater stroke, the other shoulder comes backwards past the swimmer's cheek as their arm travels through the air. Their legs do a constant kick of two, four or six kicks for each arm stroke. How many kicks they use depends on whether they are sprinting (six kicks) or swimming longer distance (two or four kicks).

Arm stroke

Backstrokers begin each stroke by putting their arm into the water, little finger first. Then they scoop the water down, out and upwards again, before sweeping down with their elbow bent until their hand comes out of the water at about hip level. The movement a backstroker makes with their hands is like a wiggly 'S' shape (looking towards their right-hand side).

When the starting gun goes off, backstroke swimmers fling themselves backwards from the wall. Their coaches teach them to try and arc smoothly into the water and to go quite deep under the surface. Once under, they are allowed to swim underwater for 15 metres before coming back to the surface. Most use as much of the distance as they can. The fastest underwater kick is a butterfly action, a bit like a dolphin flipping its tail as it swims.

Leg kick

Backstroke leg kick is very similar to front crawl. The main difference is that coaches tell the swimmers to hold their hips high, near the surface of the water. The kick is done so that their feet stay under the surface of the water.

Turns

When a backstroke swimmer is nearing the wall, they are allowed to turn on to their front and do a tumble turn, similar to a front crawl turn. But they have to push off on their back, and they must surface again within 15 metres.

Natalie Coughlin

One of the USA's brightest hopes for Olympic gold, Natalie Coughlin is among the world's top backstroke swimmers. In 2002 she was the first woman ever to break the one-minute barrier for 100m backstroke, with a time of 58.58 seconds. That same year Coughlin, who swims for the Cal Berkeley club in California, also won four gold medals at the Pan-Pacific Games.

Relays and medley races

As well as swimming individual single-stroke races, swimmers also race in relays and medley races. In relay races, four different swimmers take it in turns to swim an equal distance – usually 4 x 25m (100m), 4 x 50m (200m), 4 x 100m (400m) or 4 x 200m (800m). In medley races, swimmers swim equal distances of four different strokes – either individually or as part of a relay team.

Relays

In freestyle or front crawl relays all the swimmers do the same stroke. Medley relays are made up of all four strokes, which are swum in a particular order. The race begins with the backstroke swimmer, who goes off first because he or she would not be able to see the other swimmers arriving at the wall from any other starting place. Next is the breaststroke swimmer, who dives in just as the backstroke racer touches the wall. Then comes the butterfly leg of the relay, before finally the front crawl swimmer dives into the pool to complete the last leg.

Takeovers

Takeovers happen when one swimmer finishes their leg of the relay and another begins. The rules say that a swimmer must maintain contact with the starting blocks until the incoming swimmer has touched the wall. The ideal relay takeover is one where the outgoing swimmer has begun to dive in and has just their toes on the blocks as the incoming swimmer finishes their leg. Races are often won by as little as just one-tenth of a second, or the blink of an eye, so making the takeover as fast as possible can make all the difference.

The moment when one swimmer finishes their leg of a relay and another begins is called the takeover. The swimmer diving in makes what is called a 'flying start', although their feet are still touching the starting block. The swimmer making the flying start in the picture is Australian Kirsten Thomas in the Sydney 2000 Olympics 4 x 200m women's freestyle relay.

Medley races

As well as medley relays, swimmers also swim individual medley races, doing an equal distance of each stroke – butterfly, backstroke, breaststroke and front crawl in that order. Individual medley races are usually swum over 4 x 25m (100m), 4 x 50m (200m) or 4 x 100m (400m). In the Olympic Games and the World Championships the swimmers race in 50-metre pools, so only 4 x 50m and 4 x 100m medley races are held.

These four photos show the Chinese women's 4 x 100m medley relay team in action. The strokes are: 1) backstroke, 2) breaststroke, 3) butterfly and 4) front crawl.

Starting sequence

At the start of a race, the referee blows three short blasts on his or her whistle. This is a signal to the swimmers that they should get ready to race and stand by the starting blocks. They take off their T-shirts and get their goggles ready. Then the referee blows one long blast, and the swimmers get up on to their starting blocks and move forward into a racing crouch at the front of the blocks. (Backstroke swimmers jump into the water at this point, then grip on to their blocks ready to get into the starting position.)

Deep training

Training for swimming is as hard as for any sport in the world. Most top swimmers train for between 20 and 30 hours a week. Some of this is weight training to improve their strength, and **flexibility** work to keep them **supple**. But most of all they spend long hours ploughing up and down the training pool.

Starting out

When young people first get into swimming, their coaches don't ask them to launch straight into a 25-hour training week! Most people start by going to training two or three times a week, with each training **session** lasting an hour or so. Once swimmers start to improve, their coaches often invite them to extra training sessions. Soon the only free day they have is Saturday, when most inter-club competitions and championships are usually held. At this point, swimming has almost taken over their life.

Training fact

Most experts believe that it's not a good idea for children below the age of about 14 to do too much hard training, as it can lead to serious joint problems in later life. Despite this, many swimmers do risk injury by starting hard training sooner than this.

Top-level training

At the top level, swimmers usually start a normal day's training very early in the morning, at about 6.00 a.m. They train for up to 2 hours, then go home to rest. More training, usually out-of-the-water training such as weights, circuit training or flexibility, follows around lunchtime. Then they rest again before heading to the pool for an evening training session, to do another couple of hours of swimming.

A Japanese swimmer works with her coach during training in the Olympic Pool at the Atlanta Olympics in July 1996.

Training sessions

Training sessions usually begin with a short warm-up and stretching on the poolside. Then the coaches tell the swimmers what their water warm-up will be. Usually they swim at least 800 metres, not especially quickly but aiming to stretch their muscles and get loosened up. After the warm-up the coach tells the swimmers the first 'set' – a group of swims all done at a particular speed. For example, they might do six 100-metre swims, each starting 1 minute 10 seconds after the last. Then they will be given the next 'set', and so on.

Most top swimmers shower after training, to clean off the pool water and the chlorine smell. As well as keeping them smelling sweet, it marks a break between training and other activities, and helps their mind switch off from swimming for a while.

Most top swimmers spend many hours a day training in the pool. This takes a lot of dedication, as even world champions can get bored of swimming sometimes!

Being the best

US swimmer Jenny Thompson is one of the most successful female Olympians ever. Born in 1973 and originally from Dover, New Hampshire, Thompson now trains in New York City. As well as her Olympic medal haul, which includes eight golds, Thompson – now famous as a fearsome trainer – has won thirteen **long-course** world championship medals, five of them gold. She says, 'I love the fact that you alone are entirely accountable for your performance – you either worked hard or you didn't – the work shows up in your race result (most of the time).'

Flexibility

Top-level swimmers need to be very flexible. It is difficult to swim with good **technique** unless you have flexible muscles, especially in your neck, shoulders, lower back and legs. Because of this, many swimmers spend part of each day working on their **flexibility**. They might do this in an organized training **session**, but it could also be something they do at home, sitting in front of the television or listening to music.

Neck

A flexible neck is very important because it allows swimmers to hold their head at an unusual angle, looking ahead with their chin up. This is especially vital in front crawl and butterfly.

Shoulders

Having flexible shoulders is important because it helps swimmers to stop their body from twisting about as they swim down the pool. For instance, a freestyle swimmer with flexible shoulders will be able to make their overarm **recovery** without turning their body to the side to get their arm above the surface. This means that they make less **turbulence** and cause less **resistance** as they pass through the water, so they can swim faster as a result.

Thighs and calves

Flexible thighs and calves help swimmers do a more efficient leg kick. This is especially important in breaststroke, where most of the swimmer's speed comes from their legs.

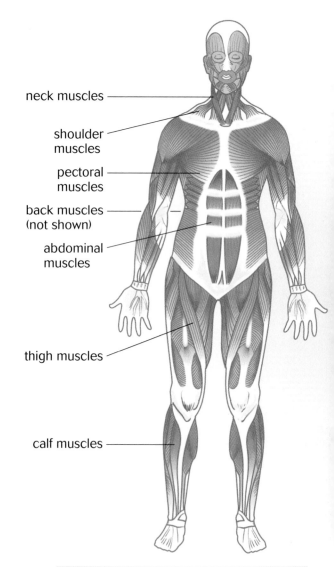

neck muscles

shoulder muscles

pectoral muscles

back muscles (not shown)

abdominal muscles

thigh muscles

calf muscles

Swimmers get a full-body workout, using practically all their muscles, in every single training session and race. The main muscles used in swimming are shown in the diagram above.

Stretching fact

The photo on the right shows US star Natalie Coughlin stretching before a race. Swimmers should remember never to stretch until it hurts the muscle they are stretching, as this could lead to injury. Instead, they should relax it as soon as it starts to feel uncomfortable.

Key flexibility facts

All swimmers need to be flexible, whichever stroke they do. They need all their muscles to be loose and able to stretch and contract into the right shapes. But some strokes require special flexibility:

• Breaststroke – the hips, groin and ankles all need to be flexible for the breaststroke leg kick. The lower back needs to be flexible to help the **torso** rise up out of the water.
• Backstroke – the neck and shoulders need to be strong and flexible to keep the head in the right position. Loose back and pectoral muscles help the arms turn over rapidly.

• Front crawl – flexible, strong neck muscles are needed to keep the head in the right position, while flexible shoulder muscles mean the arms can move through the stroke without disturbing the torso's balance in the water.
• Butterfly – nearly everything has to be flexible for butterfly, especially the neck, shoulders and lower back.

You can see from this photo of a butterfly swimmer just how flexible the neck, shoulders and back need to be!

Weight training

Almost all top swimmers today use weight training to develop specific muscles. The kind of weight training their coaches set them depends on their speciality event. Their weight training is governed not so much by the stroke they swim as the distance they specialize in. Sprinters need a different kind of muscle from distance swimmers, so sprinters need to do a different kind of weight training in order to achieve this.

This French swimmer is using weights to develop her muscles prior to competing in the 2000 Sydney Olympics.

Muscle types

Weight training uses extra strain (the weights) to develop muscles to a greater degree than normal. The muscles develop differently depending on how the weights are used. The two extremes are either short, fat muscles, which are very powerful, or long, thin muscles, which are less powerful but more flexible and able to work for longer.

Muscles for sprinting

A 100m sprint race is usually over in a minute or less. The shortest sprints, such as the 50m, take a little more than 20 seconds. They are over so quickly that some sprinters only breathe once during the race. Sprinters don't really need as much **stamina** as distance swimmers, but they do need lots of strength, to power them quickly through the water. If their muscles burn up all the available energy quickly it doesn't matter – the race will soon be over.

For this reason, sprinters use weight training to help them build up explosively powerful muscles. To do this they use heavy weights, but repeat the exercise they do relatively few times.

Muscles for distance

Distance swimmers have different needs from sprinters. Their muscles have to work over a longer period of time. Explosive, powerful muscles would burn energy too quickly, so distance swimmers use lighter weights than sprinters, but repeat the exercises more times. They add **endurance** and strength to their muscles, but not so much that they will run out of puff before the end of the race.

Australian swimming star Michael Klim (left) has the typical short, powerful muscles of a sprint swimmer. Fellow Australian Grant Hackett (right), by contrast, has the longer, slimmer muscles of a distance swimmer.

Overtraining and injuries

Training hard is important, but it is also important not to train too hard or too much. Because swimmers put in so much physical effort, it is especially important for them to allow their bodies time to recover before they go back into the pool or weights room. Otherwise they will be training when their muscles haven't yet recovered from the last **session**, and won't be able to work out at full speed. Furthermore, most swimming injuries are a result of overtraining or not warming up properly. They include torn muscles and problems with joints. Many swimmers end up with shoulder problems, and need physiotherapy or even surgery to carry on swimming.

Injury fact

Swimming injuries are rare. This is because the water supports a swimmer's body at all times, so the chances of getting an **impact injury** are small. Some people do manage to bang their head on the bottom as they dive in, which can be very serious – it can even lead to being paralysed if their spine is damaged. Backstroke swimmers sometimes bang their heads on the end of the pool because they can't see where they are going.

Mental training

At the very top level, swimming is a mental test as well as a demanding physical one. Coaches play an important part in helping swimmers take a good mental approach, by talking them through the race they are about to be in. But once the swimmers have dived into the pool to race, they are on their own.

Training

Swimming training can be quite boring – going up and down the pool, getting the distance done, for three or four hours each day. There's no one to speak to while swimming, and in the gaps between swims most people are kept busy just trying to catch their breath for the next one. Swimmers develop all sorts of ways of keeping the boredom at bay. Some people sing songs to themselves; others run through whole scripts of films or TV shows in their heads. One top junior swimmer used to run through all the US states in order, west-to-east, north-to-south.

Keeping yourself working hard in training is also very important. Sometimes just the competition of training with other people is enough to turn every training swim into a race. But at other times, many swimmers try little tricks to keep themselves as motivated as possible. Some might imagine they're coming down the last length of an Olympic final; others might pretend there's a shark behind them, to push themselves for an extra spurt of speed. Anything that can coax a little extra from tired muscles has got to be worth a try!

Members of the US women's 4 x 200m relay team cheer on their remaining swimmer at the Pan-Pacific Swimming Championships in 2002. Cheering for each other is a good way of helping the whole team feel excited and swim well.

Competition

The mental side of racing is very important. Swimmers need to hit the water feeling absolutely positive that they can clock up a good time. Coaches usually try to help their swimmers by talking through the coming race with them. They give advice on how the race should be **paced**, crucial things like starts and turns, and the tactics swimmers could use (see pages 38–39).

Targets

Most coaches agree that the best way for a swimmer to improve their swimming is to set personal targets. To start a swimming career with the aim of becoming an Olympic champion leaves a swimmer an awful long way to go before they can achieve their goal. It's better to start by wanting to knock 1 second off their personal best time. Once this is done, they can aim to knock off another half second. If they can keep shaving slivers of time from their personal best, they may one day make it to a World Championship final!

Kieren Perkins

Kieren Perkins of Australia (left) was probably the greatest-ever distance swimmer. He broke twelve world records over 400m, 800m and 1500m freestyle, and was the first person in history to hold Olympic, World, Commonwealth and Pan-Pacific titles simultaneously for the same event. Perkins won gold in the Olympics of 1992 and 1996, and then cemented his greatness with a silver in the 2000 Games.

Perkins knew the importance of being mentally prepared for an important race. He said, 'I start months before the event. I just sit there and visualize the race in my mind. I dive into the pool. I'm swimming strongly. I'm out in front. The crowd are roaring, I can hear them. No one can catch me. I even see myself up there on the dais with the gold medal placed around my neck.'

Fine tuning

Swimming coaches usually adapt their training **sessions** as big competitions loom. This is because it would be almost impossible to swim a best time in the middle of deep training. During hard training swimmers feel semi-tired for much of the time, but for an important race they need to feel full of energy. So their coaches plan their training to bring them to peak condition just at the right moment. This change in training before a big competition is called a **taper**.

Tapering

When a swimmer is tapering for an important championship, their coach will make them swim less and less distance in training as the race draws nearer and nearer. During deep training, swimmers often do lots of swims with a small gap between each one – for example, ten 100-metre swims, each starting 1 minute and 20 seconds after the last. This might leave them with just 10 seconds rest between each one.

As the competition approaches, the coaches let swimmers have more rest between each swim. They might do five 100-metre swims, going off every $2\frac{1}{2}$ minutes. This lets them have well over a minute's rest between each swim. It also means there is time for swimmers to get out of the pool and dive in instead of pushing off the wall, allowing them to practise their racing starts.

Dutch swimmer Inge de Bruijn dives in during training at the Sydney Olympics in 2000. De Bruijn was one of the successes of the Games, setting world records in the 50m and 100m freestyle.

Getting faster

The coaches expect their swimmers' times to be faster in a set with long rests than in a set with less rest. They watch the turns to make sure they're being done as fast as possible, and check that the swims are being **paced** well. Some swimmers taper so much that they might only swim a few hundred metres in the days leading to the competition, so that they conserve their energy. Tapering in this way helps bring a top swimmer to the level they need to be at in order to win races. It gets their body used to going at maximum speed, as well as the different changes of pace and accelerations out of turns that they will use in a race.

Shaving fact

Once race day comes there is one final swimming ritual almost all swimmers follow. This is called 'shaving down' and involves swimmers shaving all the hair from their bodies. Some people say that shaving down is a way of physically swimming faster, because the hairs that are removed would otherwise create drag. Others say that the feeling of water against freshly shaved skin instead creates a **psychological effect** that helps swimmers go faster, sending a message to their brain that this is a different, special situation requiring extra effort.

Michael Klim helps his Australian team-mate Adam Pine discover what he'll look like if he ever goes bald. Pine and the other swimmers are 'shaving down' – removing all their body hair before a race – and Pine has decided to lose the hair from his head, as well.

Food and diet

One of the things non-swimmers don't realize about top-level swimmers is how much they eat. Normal people need about 2000 calories a day; a swimmer in deep training eats between 5000 and 7000 calories a day. All that food takes a long time to eat!

Foods such as pasta, bread and potatoes are a useful source of carbohydrates for swimmers. Carbohydrates provide raw fuel that a swimmer's body can burn quickly when necessary.

Balanced diet

Because top athletes put their bodies under tremendous pressure, it is extra-important for them to eat the right foods. They need carbohydrates from food such as pasta, bread or potatoes, to provide raw fuel that their bodies can burn quickly when needed. It is also important for them to eat some slower-burning foods that contain fats – cheese, for example. Fresh fruit and vegetables provide vitamins and other **nutrients** that help the body to grow and to recover from hard training. Finally, protein-rich foods help with muscle recovery and growth.

Too much of any one type of food is a bad idea, so many top swimmers take the advice of nutritionists. These are experts who know how different foods work, and can advise swimmers on which foods would be best to eat during training and racing.

Competition food

Few swimmers eat a big meal just before racing. Usually they have a medium-sized meal the night before, then a light breakfast on the morning of the race. If they are racing in the morning that might be all they need; afternoon or evening races mean having a light lunch. This might be some cooked pasta, or maybe just a sandwich. Most people avoid fatty foods on race day, as these take a long time to digest and release their energy slowly, over a relatively long period of time.

Swimming and drugs

Some swimmers have used banned drugs to improve their performance. One of the most common is anabolic steroid, which allows people to train harder and build up bigger muscles than they would otherwise be able to manage. In the past, some national organizations actually encouraged their swimmers to take drugs. Many East German swimmers took steroids during the 1970s and 1980s – some were even given them by their coaches without knowing it.

The swimming authorities now work harder than ever before to clamp down on people using banned drugs. The medallists at big competitions all have tests to discover if they are using drugs. Top swimmers can also be visited at any time by officials and asked to undergo a drugs test. Anyone failing a test could be banned from competing for life.

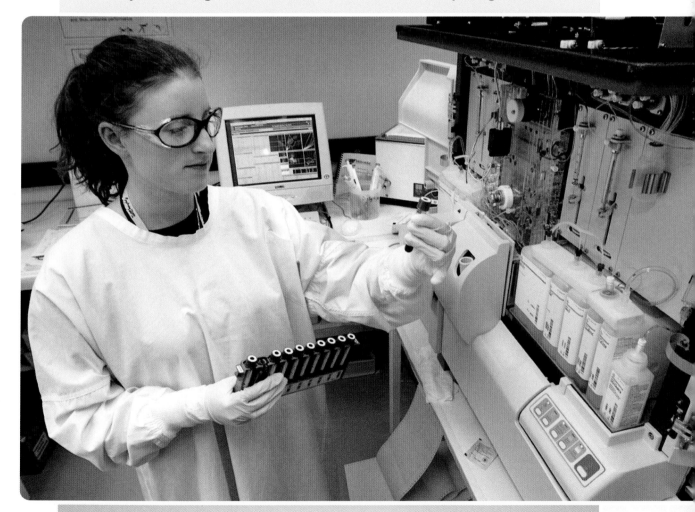

An Olympic drug-testing laboratory technician works on a blood sample taken to test for the banned drug EPO at the Sydney 2000 Olympics. EPO can be used by swimmers to artificially boost their endurance.

Swimming galas

Swimming galas are competitions between swimming clubs. They are sometimes also held between schools, colleges, regions or even countries. Each team enters its strongest swimmers in a range of events, and points are given for each place. At the end of the gala the team with the most points wins. Sometimes gala organizers give double points for relays. This can make the last relay at the end of a long gala very exciting, with more than one team able to win the gala if they win the final race.

Warming up

Each team is given its own lane to warm-up in; the 'warm-up' normally lasts half an hour. The warm-up gives swimmers a chance to loosen up their muscles. Members of the relay teams can practise their takeovers, and backstrokers get to test out how many strokes they will take from the warning flags to the end of the pool. The warm-up also allows everyone to get to know the pool, even if they have never swum there before.

Gala fact

Galas often happen while club swimmers are in deep training. Because of this they provide a good opportunity to practise starts, turns and relay takeovers. If swimmers can get these right in the middle of deep training, they have a good chance of getting them right at the big championships.

A warm-up at the 2000 Sydney Olympics. The swimmers get a chance to practise their starts and turns, as well as loosening up their muscles.

Team coaches

Once the gala begins, the whole team sits down in the same area. The races happen quite quickly one after another, so the team coaches make sure the swimmers know their race is coming up and tell them when to go and get ready. They also give the swimmers advice about how to **pace** their swim, as well as on their starts and turns. With so many people on the poolside, galas can be quite chaotic – which is all part of the fun.

Cheering

One of the best things about galas is the team spirit they create. If everyone stands up and cheers their teammates on, it makes the racing more exciting and fun. Lots of cheering also often helps swimmers to squeeze out a little bit more speed, and can make the difference between swimming an average time and a good one.

Here US swimmers are cheering on their teammates in action in the pool. Support like this can really help swimmers get the best out of themselves.

Timing

Many swimming races are very close, with just a few fractions of a second separating the first three places. In top-level competitions, each end of the pool has a touch-sensitive timing pad on it, which links to a computer that works out the racers' times. In smaller competitions timekeepers stand at the end of each lane with stopwatches, taking the times of all the racers.

Split seconds after touching the electronic timing pad, a racer looks up to check her time and position.

Championships

Big championships are the competitions that top swimmers build their training around. Someone like Lenny Krayzelburg, the American 100m backstroke world-record holder, probably started planning towards the 2004 Olympics some time in 2001. He will have other targets along the way – winning the US nationals, for example – but everything will lead towards winning an Olympic gold.

Heats, semis and finals

Major championships have heats, semi-finals and finals. Everyone races in a heat, then the fastest sixteen swimmers go into the semi-finals. The fastest eight swimmers from the two semis go into the final. Some championships don't have semis, in which case the fastest eight from the heats go straight into the final.

Semis and the final are both arranged with the fastest swimmers in the middle. This means that, if things go to form, the fastest swimmers end up racing each other for the medals in the middle lanes.

Sessions and registration

Because not all the races can fit into a single day, modern swimming championships are divided into different **sessions**. Usually the morning session is for heats, while the afternoon or evening session is for semi-finals or finals. Before the start of each session, swimmers have to register with the organizers to confirm that they are there. Usually swimmers or their team managers have to hand in a special slip of paper with their event, name and entry time listed on it.

In this photograph of a butterfly race, you can see how the racers are coming down the pool in a chevron, with the fastest ahead in the middle and the slowest behind at the sides.

Warming up

Each session begins with a warm-up. This is a chance to practise starts and turns, as well as to loosen up muscles ready for the race. Lots of swimmers also use the warm-up to check out the competition and see how they're looking. Most coaches try to discourage this – if the opposition is looking good, it's easy to be put off!

Seeding

The heats of most competitions are seeded. This means that the swimmers with the slowest entry times swim first, while those with the fastest times swim last. The idea is that everyone swims in a heat with people going at a similar speed, so the racing is closer. This makes it more likely that they will be able to push each other to a faster time.

At major championships the seeding system works differently. The last four heats have the fastest swimmers in the centre lanes. So the top seed goes in heat eight, lane four; the second seed in heat seven, lane four, the third seed in heat six, lane four and so on.

US swimmer Aaron Peirsol holds his swimming hat aloft after winning the 2003 World Championships 100m backstroke final in Barcelona, Spain.

Lane seeding fact

In semi-finals and finals the swimmers in each race are arranged in order of speed. The ordering goes like this:

Fastest	Lane 4
2nd fastest	Lane 5
3rd fastest	Lane 3
4th fastest	Lane 6
5th fastest	Lane 2
6th fastest	Lane 7
7th fastest	Lane 1
8th fastest	Lane 8

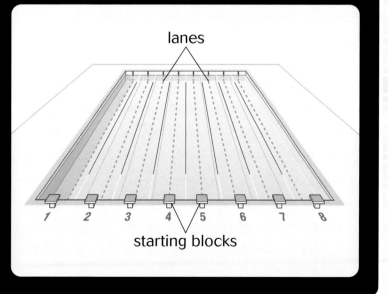

Tactics

As race day comes closer, coaches spend extra time talking about tactics. Tactics tend to concentrate on any part of the race where a winning margin could be gained. Coaches run through each race beforehand with their swimmers, making sure they know the best way to **pace** a race, where to put in maximum effort and – most important of all – where to expect the pain to start.

Sprinting

Tactics in a 50m sprint are fairly simple. Everyone just goes as fast as they can. Even in such a short race, though, the top swimmers are working to a plan. They know exactly how many strokes they will use to cover the distance, as well as where to breathe. Tactics are also important in longer, 100m sprints. Most coaches tell their swimmers not to go flat-out for the first half length – going really fast could leave them too tired to sprint at the end of the race.

Middle-distance tactics

Because there are more turns in a middle-distance race than a sprint race, turns are more important: stealing half a metre on each turn in a 400m race (in a 50-metre long pool) adds up to 3.5 metres advantage – that's two whole body lengths. Middle-distance swimmers are coached to go at a pace their coaches know they can maintain. There would be no point in winning the first 200 metres of a 400m race if it left you too tired to stay in the lead.

Mark Foster

One of the world's top sprinters is Mark Foster, from the University of Bath club in the UK. A world-record holder for 50m freestyle (**short course**), he specializes in 50m freestyle and butterfly races. His racing tactics are not especially difficult to work out: like most 50m specialists, he goes fast all the way from start to finish! Even Foster, though, admits to saving a little extra effort for the end of the race.

Medley tactics

Medley racers tend to have a good idea of how fast they can go for each stroke. The key to their race is balancing the amount of effort they put into each leg of the race, so that they don't try too hard on butterfly, for example, leaving themselves too tired when they reach the last leg. Medley swimmers usually try to measure out their energy so that the last bit is used up with the last stroke they make before they touch the wall.

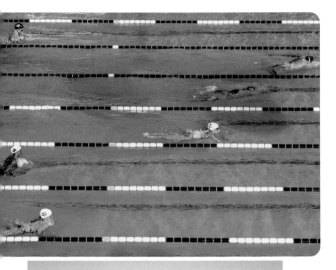

The lead can change hands several times in a medley race, as swimmers are usually better at some strokes than others.

Long-distance tactics

Long-distance race tactics are similar to medley races. The best long-distance swimmers are able to churn out length after length at almost exactly the same speed. They steadily build up a lead over people who can't quite keep up the same pace: over an 800m or 1500m race, a few fractions of a second gained on each length adds up to a big winning margin.

Relay tactics

Tactics can make a big difference in relays, and different teams take different approaches. Some coaches like to put their fastest swimmers first, hoping to build up an unbeatable lead. Others like to start with their second-fastest swimmer, put the two slower swimmers in the middle positions and have their fastest swimmer going last, so that if the finish is close they might squeeze out a win. Tactical decisions are made more complicated by the different abilities of the swimmers the coach has chosen for the team. Some people are best at coming from behind. Others like to start with a lead they can defend.

Some relay swimmers are better at standing starts; others are brilliant at flying starts like this during the middle of a race.

Major competitions

Every weekend there is a swimming competition somewhere: a club race, an inter-school match or a regional championship. But some competitions loom large in everyone's mind – these are the big ones, the races all swimmers dream of one day winning.

Olympic Games

Every four years all the major powers in world swimming gather together at the Olympic Games, the highlight of any champion swimmer's career. The Sydney Olympics in 2000 were one of the best swimming meets ever, with over 15,000 spectators packing the Olympic pool complex and creating an atmosphere that spurred the swimmers to some incredible performances.

World Championships

The annual World Swimming Championships are second only to the Olympics in the minds of most swimmers. The Championships alternate between **long-course** and **short-course** racing, with long-course competition being held in odd-numbered years. At the Championships held in Barcelona, Spain in July 2003, twelve new world records were set, and another record was equalled. Some records were broken more than once, with swimmers setting records in semi-finals that were beaten in the final. The star of the meet was Michael Phelps of the USA (see panel opposite).

Commonwealth Games

The Commonwealth Games are held every four years. The biggest swimming countries at the Games are Australia, Canada, New Zealand and the UK. Because the Australian team is there, anyone winning a gold medal will have to be a world-class swimmer!

Russian Alexander Popov was a double gold winner at the 1996 Olympics, before injury almost ended his career (see page 45). Here, he is pictured celebrating after taking gold at the 2003 World Championships.

World Cup

The World Cup is a series of races held throughout the year, at different locations around the world, in which the world's top swimmers compete for money and other prizes. The World Cup meets give everyone an idea of how their fellow swimmers are doing, as well as keeping racers sharp. In addition, swimmers get to check out venues around the world, so they're ready if a major championship is held there.

The USA's Amanda Beard displays her gold medal for the 200m breaststroke at the 2003 World Championships.

European Championships

The European Championships (held every two years) is a regional competition open only to swimmers from European countries. Most top swimmers see them as a stepping-stone to the World Championships or the Olympics.

Pan-Pacific Games

Similar to the European Championships, the Pan-Pacific Games are open only to swimmers from countries bordering the Pacific Ocean. Because Australia and the USA both take part, the standard is usually higher than in the European Championships.

Michael Phelps

Michael Phelps, from the North Baltimore swim club in the USA, is used to breaking records. In 2002 he held an amazing 20 US national age-group records, the 'youngest' being the under-11-years 100m butterfly. But at the World Championships in 2003, Phelps eclipsed all his previous achievements. By the end of the meet he held world records for 200m butterfly, plus 200m and 400m medley.

Being a champion swimmer

The life of a champion swimmer can seem pretty glamorous. The world's top swimmers – people like Ian Thorpe or Jenny Thompson, for example – are able to sign sponsorship deals with big sports companies. The companies want to be associated with the best sportspeople, and are willing to pay for the privilege. However, the reality for most top swimmers, even champions, is a bit different. Many struggle to find enough money even to pay for their accommodation, training, travel and food.

German star Franziska von Almsick is surrounded by television crews as she is interviewed during a break in training.

Training

All competition swimmers have a hard training schedule. For champions, however, life is even harder. Winning one race is relatively easy, but once you're a champion things change. Suddenly everyone wants to beat you, so there are no easy races any more if you want to stay champion. This means it becomes important to train harder than ever before. Training, resting and eating take up practically every waking hour of every single day.

Working for sponsors

Few companies are willing to sponsor a swimmer and get nothing back for their money. They want 'their' champion to be available for special events like advertising photo shoots, openings of new buildings and launches of new products. The most famous swimmers – people like Ian Thorpe – also get invited on to television talk shows, to celebrity parties and other big events. All this can take time from their training regime, making it harder for them to stay at the top.

Dawn Fraser

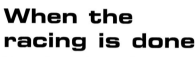

Dawn Fraser of Australia was considered to be the greatest swimmer in the world from the late 1950s until her forced retirement after the Olympic Games in 1964. She won the 100m freestyle title in three successive Games from 1956 to 1964, taking eight Olympic medals altogether. Unfortunately though, Fraser's high spirits led her into many brushes with the establishment. A prank at the Olympic Games in Tokyo brought her a 10-year suspension, subsequently reduced to 4, bringing her glittering career to an end.

When the racing is done

Very few champion swimmers continue racing over the age of 30, because by that age their bodies cannot keep up physically with younger people. Some, like Britain's Adrian Moorhouse, who won an Olympic gold medal for 100m breaststroke, go on to have media careers as commentators or writers. Others go on to work as coaches, passing on their knowledge to the champions of the future.

Many swimmers, however, give up competition and simply join the world of ordinary life: they get a job, get married, have children and become regular people. For these swimmers, it's important that they continued their education for as long as possible, so that they are able to get a decent job once the racing is over. For all former champions, whether they remain in the sport or not, there's no feeling in the world like knowing that one day they will be able to reach a dusty box off a shelf, and get out their medals to show their grandchildren.

US swimmer Amy Van Dyken signs an autograph for a young fan. Van Dyken won four Olympic golds at Atlanta in 1996.

World records

To break a world record means a great deal to many swimmers. It tells the world that they have swum faster than all their rivals and faster than the great swimmers of the past.

As training, diet and tactics have improved, world-record times have got lower and lower. Below and opposite are some selected current world records in men's and women's **long-course** events – last updated on 30 July 2003. The records are approved by FINA, the world body for swimming.

Men				
Style	**Swimmer (country)**	**Time**	**Date**	**Place**
50m Freestyle	Alexander Popov (Russia)	0:21.64	16/06/2000	Moscow, Russia
100m Freestyle	Pieter van den Hoogenband (Netherlands)	0:47.84	19/09/2000	Sydney, Australia
200m Freestyle	Ian Thorpe (Australia)	1:44.06	25/07/2001	Fukuoka, Japan
400m Freestyle	Ian Thorpe (Australia)	3:40.08	30/07/2002	Manchester, UK
800m Freestyle	Ian Thorpe (Australia)	7:39.16	24/07/2001	Fukuoka, Japan
1500m Freestyle	Grant Hackett (Australia)	14:34.56	29/07/2001	Fukuoka, Japan
50m Backstroke	Thomas Rupprath (Germany)	0:24.80	27/07/2003	Barcelona, Spain
100m Backstroke	Lenny Krayzelburg (USA)	0:53.60	24/08/1999	Sydney, Australia
200m Backstroke	Aaron Peirsol (USA)	1:55.15	20/03/2002	Minneapolis, USA
50m Breaststroke	Oleg Lisogor (Ukraine)	0:27.18	02/08/2002	Berlin, Germany
100m Breaststroke	Kosuke Kitajima (Japan)	0:59.78	21/07/2003	Barcelona, Spain
200m Breaststroke	Kosuke Kitajima (Japan)	2:09.42	24/07/2003	Barcelona, Spain
50m Butterfly	Matthew Welsh (Australia)	0:23.43	21/07/2003	Barcelona, Spain
100m Butterfly	Ian Crocker (USA)	0:50.98	26/07/2003	Barcelona, Spain
200m Butterfly	Michael Phelps (USA)	1:53.93	22/07/2003	Barcelona, Spain
200m Individual Medley	Michael Phelps (USA)	1:56.04	25/07/2003	Barcelona, Spain
400m Individual Medley	Michael Phelps (USA)	4:09.09	27/07/2003	Barcelona, Spain
4 x 100m Freestyle Relay	Australia	3:13.67	16/09/2000	Sydney, Australia
4 x 200m Freestyle Relay	Australia	7:04.66	27/07/2001	Fukuoka, Japan
4 x 100m Medley Relay	USA	3:31.54	27/07/2003	Barcelona, Spain

Women				
Style	Swimmer (country)	Time	Date	Place
50m Freestyle	Inge de Bruijn (Netherlands)	0:24.13	22/09/2000	Sydney, Australia
100m Freestyle	Inge de Bruijn (Netherlands)	0:53.77	20/09/2000	Sydney, Australia
200m Freestyle	Franziska Van Almsick (Germany)	1:56.64	03/08/2002	Berlin, Germany
400m Freestyle	Janet Evans (USA)	4:03.85	22/09/1988	Seoul, South Korea
800m Freestyle	Janet Evans (USA)	8:16.22	20/08/1989	Tokyo, Japan
1500m Freestyle	Janet Evans (USA)	15:52.10	26/03/1988	Orlando, USA
50m Backstroke	Sandra Voelker (Germany)	0:28.25	17/06/2000	Berlin, Germany
100m Backstroke	Natalie Coughlin (USA)	0:59.58	13/08/2002	USA
200m Backstroke	Kristina Egerszegi (Hungary)	2:06.62	25/08/1991	Athens, Greece
50m Breaststroke	Zoe Baker (UK)	0:30.57	30/07/2002	Manchester, UK
100m Breaststroke	Leisel Jones (Australia)	1:06.37	30/07/2003	Barcelona, Spain
200m Breaststroke	Hui Qui (China)	2:22.99	13/04/2001	Hagzhou, China
	Amanda Beard (USA)	2:22.99	25/07/2003	Barcelona, Spain
50m Butterfly	Anna-Karin Kammerling (Sweden)	0:25.57	30/07/2000	Berlin, Germany
100m Butterfly	Inge de Bruijn (Netherlands)	0:56.61	17/09/2000	Sydney, Australia
200m Butterfly	Otylia Jedrzejczak (Poland)	2:05.78	04/08/2002	Berlin, Germany
200m Individual Medley	Yanyan Wu (China)	2:09.72	17/10/1997	Shanghai, China
400m Individual Medley	Yana Klochkova (Ukraine)	4:33.59	16/09/2000	Sydney, Australia
4 x 100m Freestyle Relay	Germany	3:36.00	29/07/2002	Berlin, Germany
4 x 200m Freestyle Relay	East Germany	7:55.47	18/08/1987	Strasbourg, France
4 x 100m Medley Relay	USA	3:58.30	23/09/2000	Sydney, Australia

World record fact

Russian swimmer Alexander Popov first held a world record – for 100m freestyle – in 1994, and he went on to win gold medals at 50m and 100m freestyle at the 1996 Olympics. Before returning home, he took a holiday in Moscow, with near-tragic results. Popov was stabbed in a street brawl and almost lost his life, surviving only after 3 hours of emergency surgery. His career appeared over, but Popov came back to set a new world record for 50m freestyle in 2000. His comeback continued at Barcelona in 2003, when he won World Championships gold in both the 50m and 100m freestyle.

Glossary

endurance
the ability to carry on doing a physical activity for a long time

flexibility
the ability to stretch or move easily into a variety of different positions

flying start
the dive swimmers do if they are going second, third or fourth in a relay race. They begin to move on the blocks before the incoming swimmer has finished, so their dive is called a flying start. However, their feet must still be touching the blocks when the incoming swimmer touches the wall.

full stroke
swimming using both the arm and leg movements of a stroke together

impact injury
an injury caused by hitting something

long course
races swum in a 50-metre pool are called long-course races

nutrients
substances in foods that the body needs to survive and grow

pace/paced
the speed at which something is done is called its pace. A paced swim would be done at speeds that had been decided by the swimmer and their coach before the race began. For example, the first 50 metres in 25.5 seconds and the second 50 metres in 27 seconds, to give a total time of 52.5 seconds.

psychological effect
an effect that is in the mind, but which can still influence the body

pull
the part of the arm stroke in swimming where the swimmers 'grip' the water and pull themselves forward

recovery
the part of a swimming arm stroke that brings a swimmer's hands back to their starting position

resistance
the amount of force that stops something moving forwards

sessions
separate parts of a training or racing event

short course
races swum in a 25-metre pool are called short-course races

stamina
the ability to do something over a long period of time

supple
another word for flexible; able to stretch easily into a variety of positions

taper
a period of time spent getting physically and mentally ready for an important race

technique
the way in which something is done

torso
the main part of the human body, to which the arms, legs and neck are joined

turbulence
disturbance in the water that slows a swimmer down. Many swimmers also call this 'drag'.

Resources

Further reading

Activators: Swimming, Clive Gifford (Hodder Children's Books, 1998).

This handbook on swimming contains advice on how to perfect the different strokes. It also looks at fitness, diving and competition swimming.

Swimming and How to Improve Your Style, Paul Mason (Tick Tock, 2001).

This book provides detailed descriptions of techniques, starts and turns, as well as some excellent sequenced photos.

The Fit Swimmer, Marianne Brems (McGraw Hill, 1984).

This book suggests a variety of training sessions and techniques for making the training process more interesting.

Total Immersion: The Revolutionary Way to Swim Better, Faster and Easier, Terry Laughlin (Fireside, 1996)

Though controversial, this book encourages all swimmers to examine their technique on a day-to-day basis to see if there is room for them to improve.

Websites

http://www.fina.org – the home site of the world governing body for swimming, which also gives details of world records and championship results such as the Olympics.

http://www.britishswimming.org – the home site of the British Amateur Swimming Association.

http://www.swimming.org.au – the website of the Australian national swimming organization, this excellent site has biographies of great Australian swimmers, details of events and races, and much more.

http://www.usswim.org – this website is the home of the US national body for swimming. It is full of features, including coaching tips, biographies of stars, results from competitions as they happen, and more.

http://www.swimnews.com – a useful website containing up-to-date world swimming news.

http://www.swiminfo.com – another useful swimming website that is always well worth a look.

http://www.olympic.org – the official website of the Olympic Games.

Disclaimer

All the Internet addresses (URLs) given in this book were valid at the time of going to press. However, due to the dynamic nature of the Internet, some addresses may have changed, or sites may have changed or ceased to exist since publication. While the author and Publishers regret any inconvenience this may cause readers, no responsibility for any such changes can be accepted by either the author or the Publishers.

Index

Titles in the *Making of a Champion* series include:

Hardback   0 431 18924 2

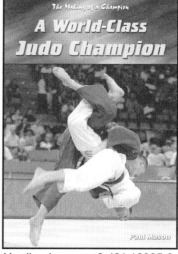

Hardback   0 431 18925 0

Hardback   0 431 18923 4

Hardback   0 431 18926 9

Hardback   0 431 18921 8

Hardback   0 431 18922 6

Find out about the other Heinemann Library titles on our website www.heinemann.co.uk/library